7/09

-2

Counting by: Fives

Esther Sarfatti

Rourke
Publishing LLC
Vero Beach, Florida 32964

www.rourkepublishing.com

PHOTO CREDITS: © Scott Waite: page 3; © Renee Brady: page 5; © Joe Cicak: page 7; © Sandra O'Claire: page 9; © Sean Locke: page 13; © Pathathai Chungyam: page 15; © Jim Jurica: page 17; © Dave Logan: page 19; © BTina Rencelj: page 21; © Denise Crew: page 23.

Editor: Robert Stengard-Olliges

Cover design by Nicola Stratford.

Library of Congress Cataloging-in-Publication Data

Sarfatti, Esther.
 Counting by : fives / Esther Sarfatti.
    p. cm. -- (Concepts)
 ISBN 978-1-60044-521-7 (Hardcover)
 ISBN 978-1-60044-662-7 (Softcover)
 1. Counting--Juvenile literature. I. Title.
 QA113.S355 2008
 513.2'11--dc22
                              2007014034

Printed in the USA

CG/CG

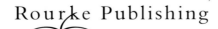

Rourke Publishing

www.rourkepublishing.com – rourke@rourkepublishing.com
Post Office Box 3328, Vero Beach, FL 32964

This is five.

What comes in fives?

Five

5

5

Five

five

5

5

A starfish has five arms.

A foot has five toes.

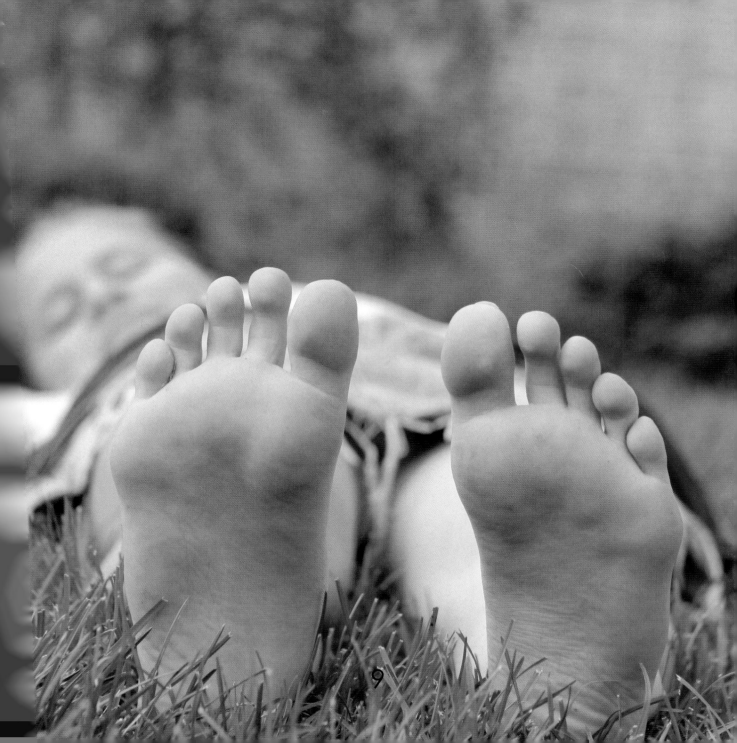

A pentagon has five sides.

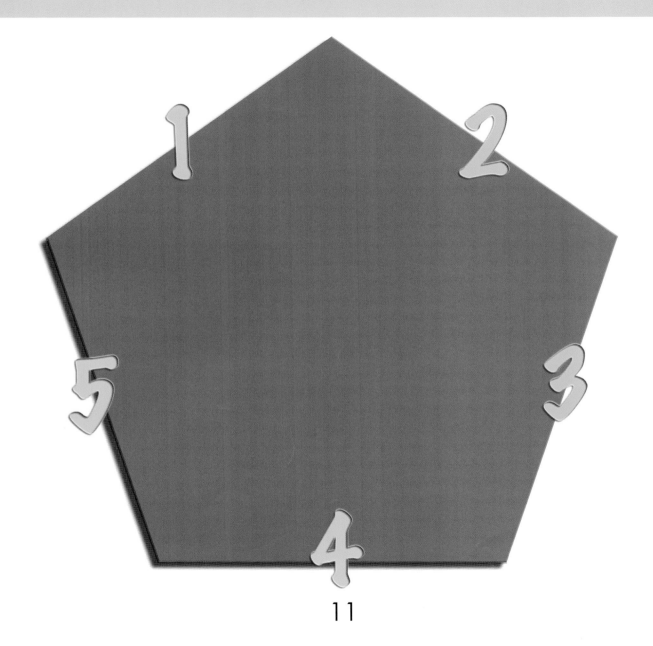

11

A week has five school days.

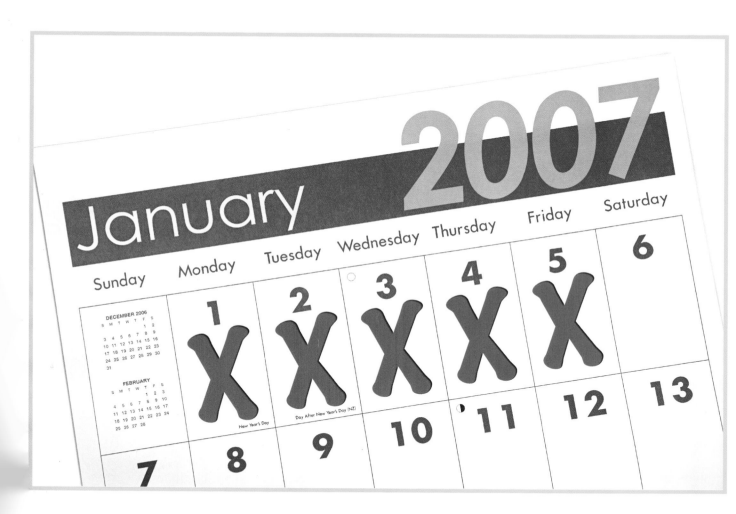

These girls have five popsicles.

15

This cake has five candles.

17

These stars have five points.

These are five dogs.

These five kids are playing.
Counting by fives is fun!

Index

cake   16
dogs   20
starfish   6
week   12

Further Reading

Dahl, Michael. *Lots of Ladybugs: Counting by Fives.*
  Picture Window Books, 2005.
Dahl, Michael. *Hands Down: Counting by Fives.* Picture
  Window Books, 2006.

Recommended Websites

www.edhelper.com/kindergarten/Number_5.htm
www.enchantedlearning.com/languagebooks/spanish/
  numbers/

About the Author

Esther Sarfatti has worked with children's books for over
15 years as an editor and translator. This is her first series
as an author. Born in Brooklyn, New York, and brought
up in a trilingual home, Esther currently lives with her
husband and son in Madrid, Spain.